Maths Adventures
Airline Pilot

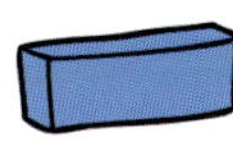

John Allan

CONTENTS

NUMERACY WORK COVERED IN THIS BOOK

CALCULATIONS:
Throughout this book there are opportunities to practice **addition, subtraction, multiplication,** and **division** using both mental calculation strategies and pencil and paper methods.

NUMBERS AND THE NUMBER SYSTEM:
- COMPARING and ORDERING NUMBERS: pages 6, 8, 18
- FRACTIONS: pages 10, 14
- READING NUMBERS IN WORDS AND FIGURES: page 6

SOLVING "REAL-LIFE" PROBLEMS:
- CALCULATION: pages 8, 10, 12, 14, 16, 18, 21, 22
- MEASUREMENTS: pages 11, 12, 14, 16, 18, 22, 24
- TIME: pages 12, 17, 21, 22, 23, 24

HANDLING DATA:
- BAR CHARTS: page 8
- BAR LINE CHARTS: page 24
- USING TABLES/CHARTS/DIAGRAMS: pages 10, 11, 12, 14, 18

MEASUREMENTS:
- VOCABULARY (time): pages 14, 16, 17, 22, 23, 24

SHAPES AND SPACE:
- 2-D SHAPES: page 27
- 3-D SHAPES: page 14
- COMPASS DIRECTIONS: page 12
- GRID COORDINATES: page 26

Copyright © 2020 Hungry Tomato Ltd

First published in 2020 by
Hungry Tomato Ltd.,
F1, Old Bakery Studios, Blewetts Wharf,
Malpas Road, Truro, Cornwall, TR1 1QH, UK

ISBN 978-1-913077-84-6

Printed and bound in China

www.hungrytomato.com

Maths is Fun

Maths is important in the lives of people everywhere. Maths is used to play games, ride bikes, go shopping—in fact, all the time! Everyone needs to use maths at work. A pilot uses maths to fly an airliner! Use real-life data and facts about planes and the work of airline pilots to practice your maths and numeracy skills. And, experience the thrill of what it's really like to fly the amazing Airbus A380.

This exciting maths book is very easy to use—check out what's inside!

The Amazing Airbus A380

This incredible plane is the largest passenger airliner in the world. It flies at MACH 0.85—this means it travels at 85% of the speed of sound. The tail of an Airbus A380 is about the same height as a six-story building, and its wings are so large that 45 family cars could park on them! Pilots have to arrive at the airport at least 80 minutes before a flight to carry out their preflight preparations.

> Fun-to-read information about airliners and the work of airline pilots.

PREFLIGHT TASKS

Before a flight, one of the pilots must walk around the plane making a detailed series of checks. This is called a walk-around. Make some checks on your plane by working out these **fractions** and divisions. Use the Airbus A380 information in the DATA BOX.

5 One **half of the tyres** on the plane's wheels need replacing. How many is that?

6 How many ladders, each eight feet long, have to be clipped together to reach the top of the plane's tail?

7 **Four cleaners** are polishing the insides of the plane's windows. How many do they each clean?

8 The plane's fuel tanks are half full of fuel. How many more gallons of fuel are needed to fill the plane's tanks?

9 How many in-flight magazines are needed for all of the passenger seats?

(You will find TIPS to help you with these questions on page 28.)

MATHS ACTIVITIES

To answer some of the questions, you will need to collect data from a DATA BOX. Sometimes you will need to collect facts and data from the text or from charts and diagrams.

You might also need a pen, pencil, and a notebook for some of the workings and answers.

PILOT FACT

Here are some of the checks pilots need to make during their walk-around:
- Check there are no dead birds trapped inside the engines.
- Make sure the **fuselage** skin is in an acceptable condition and that tyres are not worn.
- Check that the lights on the wings, flap, and tailfin are working.

DATA BOX · **AIRBUS A380**

Maximum takeoff mass (weight)	1,234,588 pounds	Total number of windows	220
Operating empty mass (weight)	1,344,819 pounds	Total number of wheels	22
Maximum **fuel capacity**	69,350 gallons	Crew	3 flight deck crew
Average fuel burn	3995 lb/hr per engine		21 **cabin** crew (flight attendants)
Maximum **range**	8,400 nautical miles (nm)		
Typical **cruising** speed	570 mph	Passenger capacity	Standard 3 class arrangement:
Engines	4 x 84,000 lbf* jet engines		14 first class passengers
Dimensions	261 ft **wingspan**		76 business class passengers
	240 ft overall length		538 economy class passengers
	80 ft tail height		

*lbf (pound of force)—a measurement of the amount of thrust force from a plane's engine.

A380 FACT

The ideal wingspan of an A380 is 300 feet, but most airports couldn't handle this size. So, it was reduced to 261 feet.

Some A380s even have private appartments for passengers.

10 **THE WALK-AROUND**

Carry out a walk-around of an A380. Walk from the aircraft's nose to the wings, along under one wing, then back. Then under the other wing and back. Finally, walk to the tip of the tail.

Approximately how far have you walked?

(Use the plane's measurements in the DATA BOX.)

11

FASCINATING FACTS ABOUT PLANES AND FLYING.

Learning to Fly an Airliner

Trainee pilots are called cadets and they learn to fly using *FLIGHT SIMULATORS*. Cadets have to sit examinations and spend 200 hours flying real planes before they can graduate. To become a pilot you need to study AERODYNAMICS, NAVIGATION, radio communication, and even METEOROLOGY. During their careers, pilots learn to fly lots of different aircraft.

1 ASSESSING THE PILOT CADET

The DATA BOX gives information on four COMMERCIAL AIRLINERS. Work out which of the four aircraft have been programmed into the flight simulator for your training flight. (You need to compare the aircraft).

- It has a WINGSPAN that is less than the wingspan of the Boeing 777.
- It has a RANGE greater than the Airbus A320.
- It is **third largest** in order of tail height.
- It is smallest in order of takeoff mass (weight).
- It has engines that are **approximately 22,500 lbf***.

Which aircraft is programmed into the flight simulator?

(You will find information about UNITS OF MEASUREMENT on page 29.)

FLIGHT TRAINING FACT

Flight simulators are machines that use computer programmes to create flying conditions just like the real thing. Pilots use flight simulators to practice taking off and landing, and to perfect dealing with **turbulence**, **thunderstorms**, and emergencies, such as an engine failure!

2 FUEL CAPACITY

Which of these is the maximum fuel capacity of the Airbus A320?
a) Five thousand, two hundred and eight gallons
b) Five thousand, two hundred and forty eight gallons
c) Five hundred and twenty four gallons

(You will find a TIP to help you with this question on page 28.)

Airbus A320

Max takeoff mass (weight)	162,000 pounds
Max fuel capacity	5,248 gallons
Max range	3,050 statute miles (sm)
Typical cruising speed	530 mph
Engines	2 x 23,800 lbf* jet engines
Dimensions	34 m wingspan
	37 m overall length
	12 m tail height

Airbus A340

Max takeoff mass (weight)	606,000 pounds
Max fuel capacity	4,127 gallons
Max range	9,200 statute miles (sm)
Typical cruising speed	555 mph
Engines	4 x 32,600 lbf* jet engines
Dimensions	60 m wingspan
	59 m overall length
	16 m tail height

Boeing 737

Max takeoff mass (weight)	143,000 pounds
Max fuel capacity	5,568 gallons
Max range	3,510 statute miles (sm)
Typical cruising speed	530 mph
Engines	2 x 22,700 lbf* jet engines
Dimensions	34 m wingspan
	31 m overall length
	13 m tail height

Boeing 777

Max takeoff mass (weight)	660,000 pounds
Max fuel capacity	5,703 gallons
Max range	6,850 statute miles (sm)
Typical cruising speed	560 mph
Engines	2 x 94,600 lbf* jet engines
Dimensions	60 m wingspan
	74 m overall length
	18 m tail height

*lbf (pound of force)—a measurement of the amount of thrust force from an engine.

Travelling the World

Airline pilots are able to fly into any airport in the world. They use special charts, called Jeppesen Charts, that show the length and width of the runways and details about the height and location of any mountains or tall buildings in the area. The plane is about to land at Hartsfield-Jackson Atlanta International Airport—the busiest airport in the world! Over 63,000 people work at Hartsfield, and flights take off and land 24 hours a day.

3 AIRPORT FACTS

The DATA BOX shows the enormous numbers of passengers that pass through the world's busiest airports every year. The passenger numbers for six of the airports have been put into a **BAR CHART**, but the airport name labels are missing.

Can you work out which bar stands for which airport? (To get you started, the red bar represents the number of passengers going through Los Angeles International Airport.)

(You will find TIPS to help you with this activity on page 28.)

DATA BOX

WORLD'S TOP 10 BUSIEST AIRPORTS

Number of passengers per year:

1st	Hartsfield International, Atlanta, USA	107,000,000
2nd	Beijing Capital, Chaoyang Shunyi, China	101,000,000
3rd	Dubai, Garhoud, Dubai	89,000,000
4th	Los Angeles International, Los Angeles, USA	88,000,000
5th	Tokyo Haneda, Ota, Japan	87,000,000
6th	O'Hare International Chicago, USA	83,000,000
7th	London Heathrow, London, UK	80,000,000
8th	Hong Kong Chek Lap Kok Island, China	75,000,000
9th	Shanghai International Pudong, China	74,000,000
10th	Paris Charles de Gaulle, Paris, France	72,000,000

4 NUMBER OF PASSENGERS

What do you need to do to work out how many passengers pass through each of the airports in a week?

(You will find a TIP to help you with this question on page 28.)

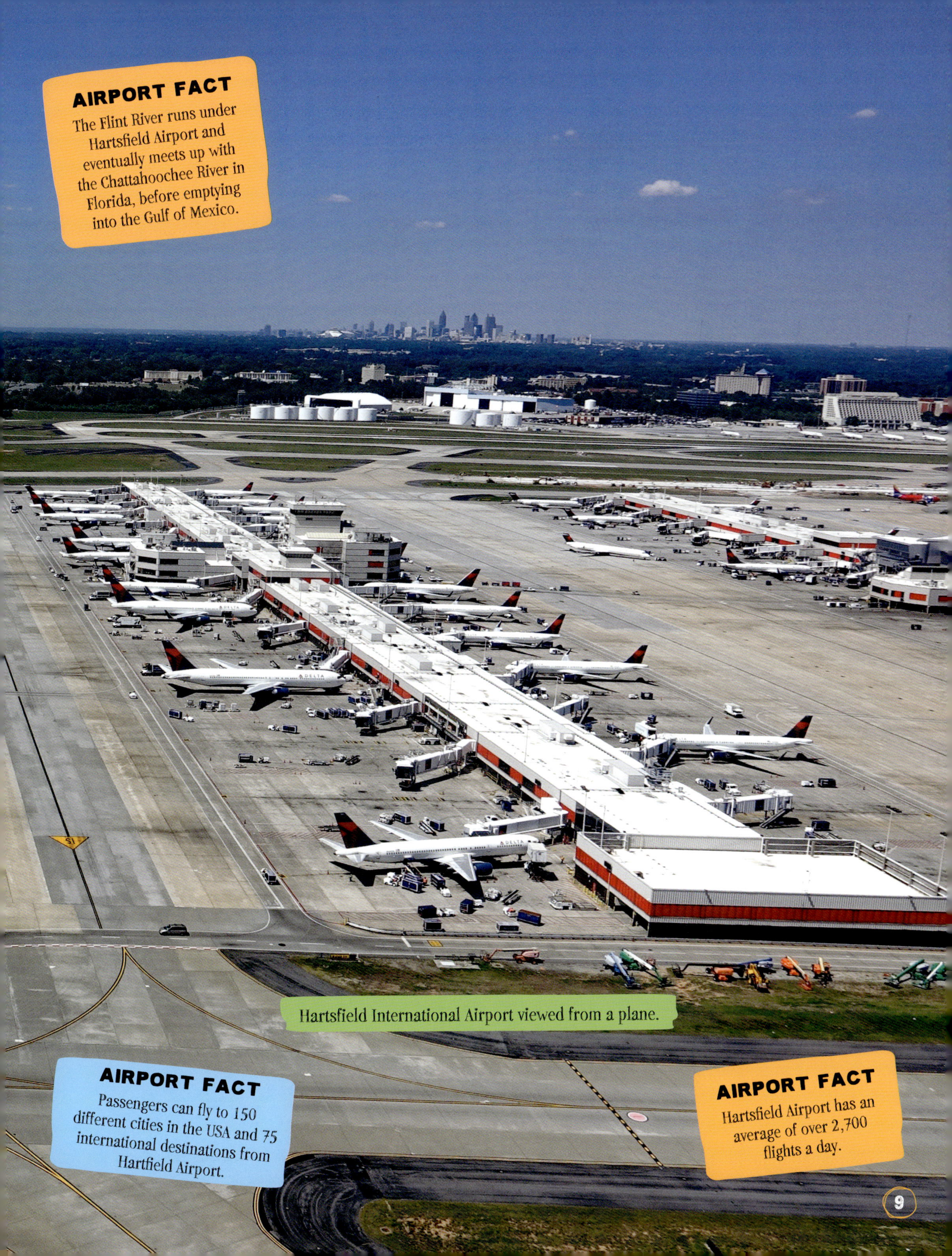

AIRPORT FACT

The Flint River runs under Hartsfield Airport and eventually meets up with the Chattahoochee River in Florida, before emptying into the Gulf of Mexico.

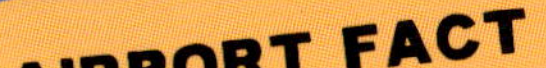

Hartsfield International Airport viewed from a plane.

AIRPORT FACT

Passengers can fly to 150 different cities in the USA and 75 international destinations from Hartfield Airport.

AIRPORT FACT

Hartsfield Airport has an average of over 2,700 flights a day.

The Amazing Airbus A380

This incredible plane is the largest passenger airliner in the world. It flies at MACH 0.85—this means it travels at 85% of the speed of sound. The tail of an Airbus A380 is about the same height as a six-story building, and its wings are so large that 45 family cars could park on them! Pilots have to arrive at the airport at least 80 minutes before a flight to carry out their preflight preparations.

PREFLIGHT TASKS

Before a flight, one of the pilots must walk around the plane making a detailed series of checks. This is called a walk-around. Make some checks on your plane by working out these FRACTIONS and divisions. Use the Airbus A380 information in the DATA BOX.

5 One **half of the tyres** on the plane's wheels need replacing. How many is that?

6 How many ladders, each eight feet long, have to be clipped together to reach the top of the plane's tail?

7 **Four cleaners** are polishing the insides of the plane's windows. How many do they each clean?

8 The plane's fuel tanks are half full of fuel. How many more gallons of fuel are needed to fill the plane's tanks?

9 How many in-flight magazines are needed for all of the passenger seats?

(You will find TIPS to help you with these questions on page 28.)

PILOT FACT

Here are some of the checks pilots need to make during their walk-around:

- Check there are no dead birds trapped inside the engines.
- Make sure the **fuselage** skin is in an acceptable condition and that tyres are not worn.
- Check that the lights on the wings, flap, and tailfin are working.

DATA BOX AIRBUS A380

Maximum takeoff mass (weight)	1,234,588 pounds	Total number of windows	220
Operating empty mass (weight)	1,344,819 pounds	Total number of wheels	22
Maximum **fuel capacity**	69,350 gallons	Crew	3 flight deck crew
Average fuel burn	3995 lb/hr per engine		21 **cabin** crew (flight attendants)
Maximum **range**	8,400 nautical miles (nm)		
Typical **cruising speed**	570 mph	Passenger capacity	Standard 3 class arrangement:
Engines	4 x 84,000 lbf* jet engines		14 first class passengers
Dimensions	261 ft **wingspan**		76 business class passengers
	240 ft overall length		538 economy class passengers
	80 ft tail height		

*lbf (pound of force)—a measurement of the amount of thrust force from a plane's engine.

A380 FACT

The ideal wingspan of an A380 is 300 feet, but most airports coudn't handle this size. So, it was reduced to 261 feet.

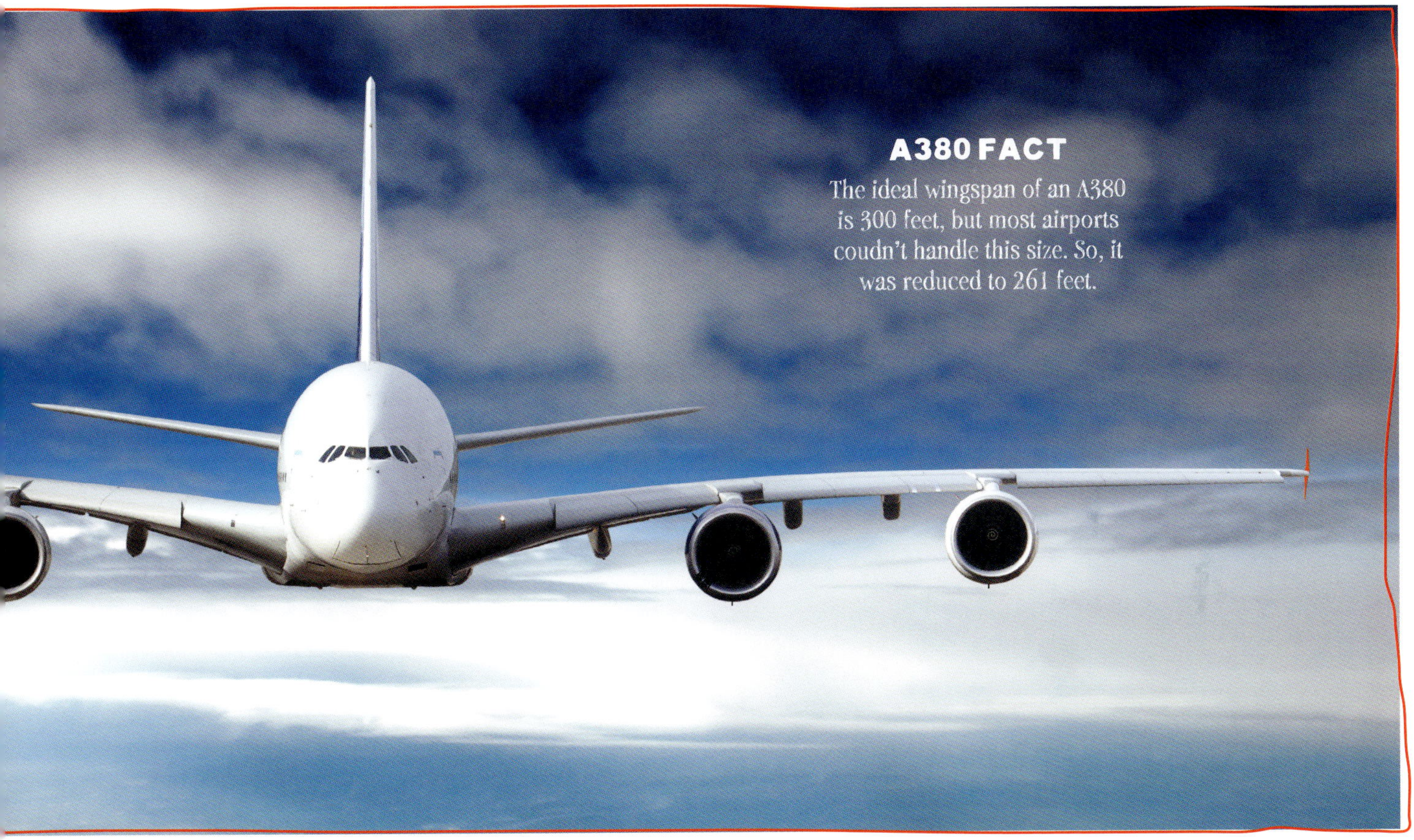

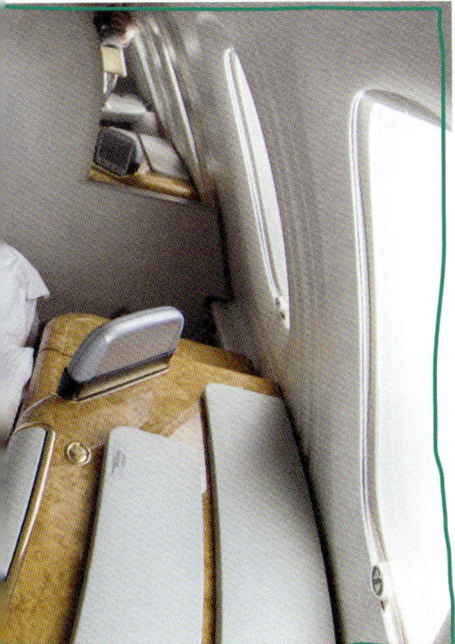

Some A380s even have private appartments for passengers.

10 THE WALK-AROUND

Carry out a walk-around of an A380. Walk from the aircraft's nose to the wings, along under one wing, then back. Then under the other wing and back. Finally, walk to the tip of the tail.

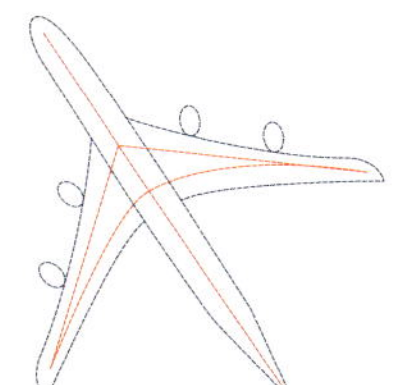

Approximately how far have you walked?

[Use the plane's measurements in the DATA BOX.]

Making a Flight Plan

ne of the most important preflight jobs that a pilot does is prepare a **FLIGHT PLAN**. The pilots need to produce a flight plan from Heathrow Airport in London to John F. Kennedy Airport (JFK) in New York City. The flight plan shows key information about the flight, such as how much fuel will be used, the speed that the plane will travel at, the direction of the wind, and how long the flight will take. The information in the flight plan is loaded onto the plane's computer system.

THE FLIGHT PLAN

The map and DATA BOX on these pages show the types of information that pilots use to help them plan their flights. Using the journey times and distances in the DATA BOX, work out the answers to these questions:

11 How much further is it in miles from Paris to Cairo than from Moscow to Rome?

12 What is the difference in journey time between New York to Los Angeles and Los Angeles to Atlanta?

13 You are planning to fly from London to Cairo via Paris. What is the distance you will travel?

You are flying from London to Atlanta, via New York and Los Angeles.

14 How far will you travel?

15 What is the total journey time?

(You will find a TIP to help you with questions 12 and 15 on page 28.)

WHICH CITY?

Use the compass on the map to answer the following questions:

16 Which cities on the map are south-west of Washington?

17 Which city on the map is north-east of Rome?

18 Which cities on the map are south-east of Paris?

FLIGHT FACT

Pilots are trained to fly around the world using air corridors—imaginary roads in the sky.

DATA BOX — FLIGHT TIMES AND DISTANCES

Journey	Distance (miles)	Journey time
London to New York	3,444	6 hours
New York to Boston	186	30 minutes
New York to Washington	228	45 minutes
New York to Los Angeles	2,471	4 hours 30 minutes
Los Angeles to Atlanta	1,944	3 hours 40 minutes
London to Paris	216	23 minutes
Paris to Cairo	2,363	4 hours 15 minutes
Moscow to Rome	1,893	3 hours 30 minutes

Preflight Check Calculations

During their preflight preparations, pilots must calculate how much fuel they will need for the journey. An A380 has an incredible *CRUISING SPEED* of 570 mph. At this speed, the plane's four engines will burn approximately 26,455 pounds of fuel every hour. A normal car would have to drive at top speed, non-stop, day and night, for over a month to use as much fuel as an A380 uses in one hour! All aircraft must carry enough fuel to reach their destination as well as spare fuel in case there is an emergency and the flight is diverted to another airport.

CHECKING THE FUEL

- The A380 burns 26,440 pounds of fuel per hour.

- It will take 6 hours to travel from Heathrow Airport, London to JFK Airport, New York.

19 What weight of fuel will it use or burn?

- If there is an emergency at JFK, you may be diverted to an airport in Boston or Washington.

20 If you divert to Boston Logan Airport, you will need fuel for a further half hour. What weight of fuel is that?

21 If you divert to Washington Dulles Airport, you will need fuel for an extra three-quarters of an hour. What weight of fuel is that?

Maintenance crew check the undercarriage of an A380.

THE CARGO HOLD

The cargo hold loaders are loading the plane. They have started stacking some CUBE-shaped boxes.

How many boxes do you think there are in each stack?

22 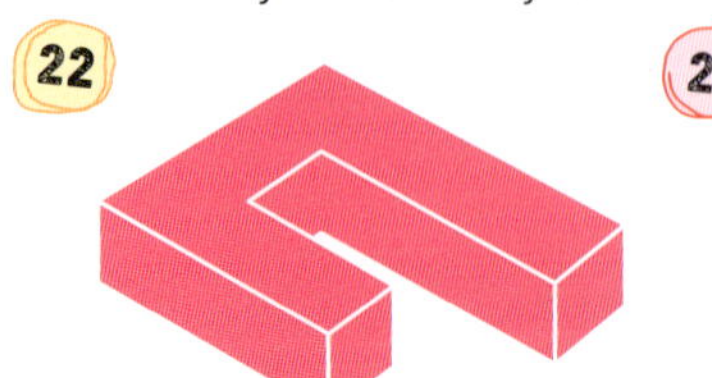

23 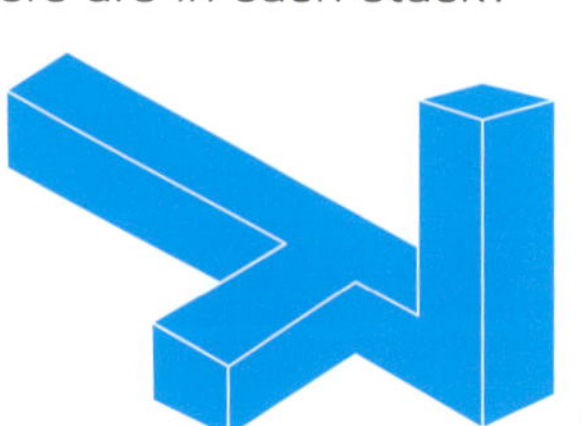

(You will find a TIP to help you with this question on page 28.)

CARGO FACT

The cargo that planes carry can include almost anything—computers, car parts, fresh fruit and flowers, silver or gold, and valuable antiques. Passengers' pets are placed in the cargo hold, sometimes with wild animals, such as cheetahs, lions, snakes, and rhinos!

A view of the cockpit in an A380

Final Check Before Takeoff

The flight plan has been completed, the fuel calculated, the weather forecasts examined and the aircraft checked—both the outside of the plane and the FLIGHT INSTRUMENTS in the COCKPIT. The two pilot seats have the same controls, but today the captain is PNF (Pilot Not Flying). This means the copilot is PF (Pilot Flying) and will take control of the plane!

HOW HEAVY?

The most the aircraft and its contents can weigh at takeoff is 1,234,588 lb. The plane must not be overloaded!

- The empty plane weighs 610,680 lb.
- You have filled up with 546,740 lb of fuel.

24 What is the weight of the empty plane and its fuel?

25 What is the maximum that the cargo, passengers and crew can now weigh?

- When your plane takes off, it will climb 3000 ft every minute.

26 How high will you be after 5 minutes?

27 How high will you be after 10 minutes?

28 After 12 minutes, the plane levels out. What is the plane's altitude (height above ground level)?

TAKEOFF PROCEDURE

- The captain tells the crew to prepare for takeoff.
- The captain and copilot run through the takeoff briefing. This includes all the normal procedures and actions to be taken if there is an emergency.
- The **CONTROL TOWER** clears the aircraft for takeoff.
- The aircraft is lined up with the runway center line.
- Takeoff **THRUST** is set on all engines.
- Within 25 seconds, the plane is travelling at 160 mph. The pilot pulls back on the controls and the aircraft's nose lifts off the runway.
- The plane is airborne. As it climbs, the plane will be travelling at 435 mph!

HOW FAR?

You are flying at 420 mph (that's 420 miles in 60 minutes).

29 How far do you travel in 1 minute?

30 How far do you travel in 12 minutes?

(You will find a TIP to help you with these questions on page 28.)

A380 FACT

During an evacuation testing, 853 passengers (the maximum number of people an A380 can hold) and 20 crew attempted to exit the aircraft in less than 90 seconds. They all got out in 78 seconds, using just 8 of the 16 exits.

An A380 taxis onto the runway

Airliners wait in a queue to be cleared for takeoff

Leaving the ground

In-flight Service

Once the aircraft is at cruising speed and the journey is underway, the passengers will relax. They will watch TV and enjoy some refreshments. The flight attendants will be busy in the galley (the plane's kitchen), heating up and preparing the meals that were loaded on board the plane. Other flight attendants serve the food and fetch drinks for all the passengers. During a flight, the attendants will also bring the flight crew drinks and food. The pilots will take it in turn to stop work and have something to eat.

FLIGHT ATTENDANTS FACT

Flight attendants don't just serve food and drinks to the passengers. They make sure that all the plane's safety rules are followed and will help passengers if there is an emergency situation.

FOOD AND DRINK

A380s carry a lot of food and drink. In the DATA BOX you will see a list of items that an A380 can carry. Use this information to answer these questions:

31 In total, how many bottles of tonic water and diet tonic water are there in the galley?

32 Ten bottles of bitter lemon are sold. What **volume** of bitter lemon is that?

33 In total, how many cartons of fruit juice are there in the galley?

34 One quarter of all the apple juice is drunk during a flight. How many millilitres is that?

35 How many more bottles of sparkling water than club soda are on board?

Check your knowledge of the signs for "less than" and "greater than." Are these statements true or false?

36 Number of cartons of orange juice > number of cartons of tomato juice.

37 Number of diet tonic waters < number of ginger ales.

38 Number of tonic waters (regular and diet) > number of sodas.

(You will find a TIP to help you with questions 36, 37, and 38 on page 28.)

Flight attendants help passengers before take-off

"

Luxury suites for first class passengers

Business class seats fold down to flat beds

Economy class seats on an A380

IN THE GALLEY

SOFT DRINKS		(all 300 ml bottles)
Soda	283	bottles
Diet soda	179	bottles
Bitter lemon	24	bottles
Club soda	75	bottles
Tonic water	143	bottles
Diet tonic water	99	bottles
Sparkling water	189	bottles
Ginger ale	108	bottles
Lemonade	124	bottles
FRUIT JUICES		(all 900 ml cartons)
Orange juice	100	cartons
Apple juice	60	cartons
Tomato juice	40	cartons

HOT DRINKS

- 240 large tea bags
- 155 packets of coffee
- Each packet of coffee makes a 1 litre pot of coffee or tea
- Each 1 litre pot gives 10 cups of tea or coffee

IN-FLIGHT FACT

The latest A380s have luxury suites for two people with double beds. There are also showers for first and business class passengers.

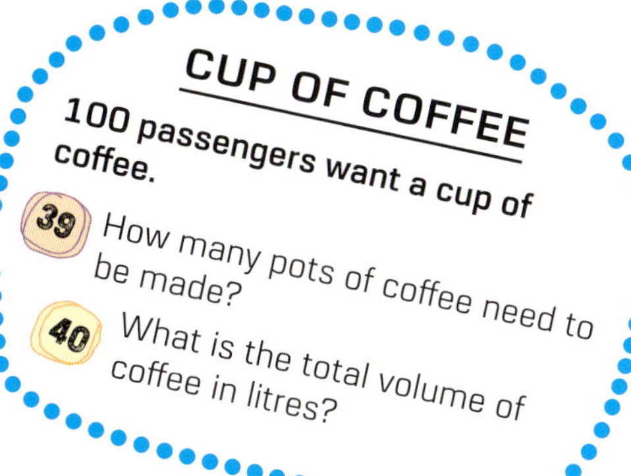

CUP OF COFFEE

100 passengers want a cup of coffee.

39 How many pots of coffee need to be made?

40 What is the total volume of coffee in litres?

Weather Warning

During a flight, pilots need to carry out a number of routine checks. Sometimes the checks show a change in the wind speed outside. This could affect the cruising speed of the plane, making it slower or faster. If the wind speed increases and there is a following wind (blowing in the same direction as the plane), the aircraft travels faster and uses less fuel. If the cruising speed drops, it will take the plane longer to reach its destination. Sometimes, a really bad storm will show on the weather RADAR. It is best to divert around storms, but this uses more fuel. Pilots have to be ready to deal with unexpected situations and make quick in-flight calculations.

THE ROUTE GAME

This game is based on an air corridor (route) between London and New York. As you play the game, you need to make some quick calculations.

- Find a dice and something that can be used as a counter.
- Start from TAKE OFF LONDON with 50 units of fuel.
- Throw the dice and move the counter the number of places shown. If you land on a LOSE or GAIN circle, change the fuel units total by the amount shown.
- Toward the end of the journey, a pilot must be cleared to land. To land at NEW YORK you need to throw the exact number. If you throw a higher number, landing has not been cleared and 2 fuel units needs to be deducted. Keep going until you throw the right number!
- How much fuel do you have left at the end?
- Now try this activity again.
- You will probably have to make different calculations and will have different levels of fuel left when you land.

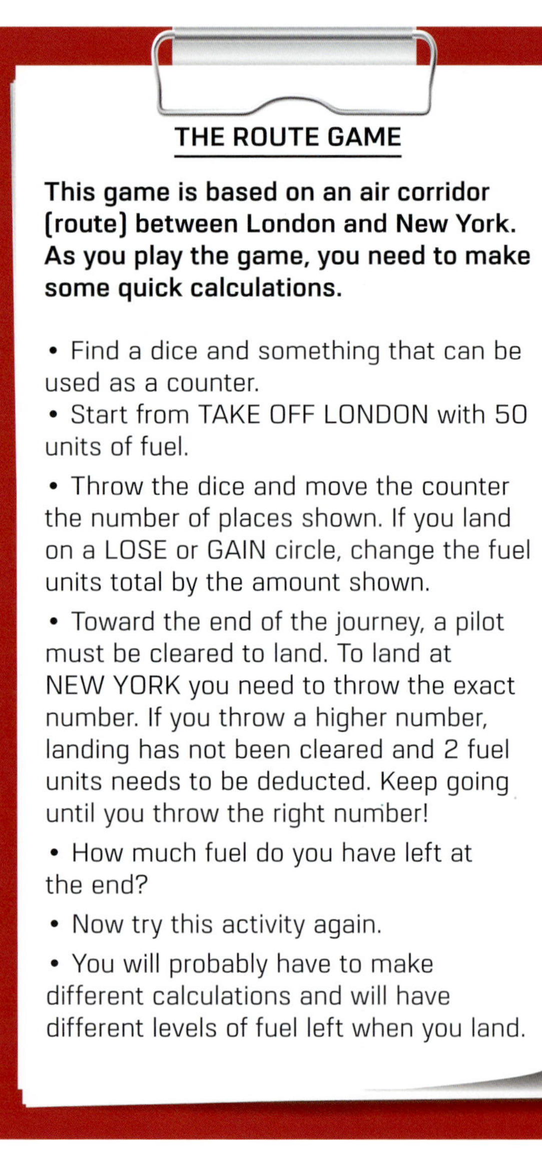

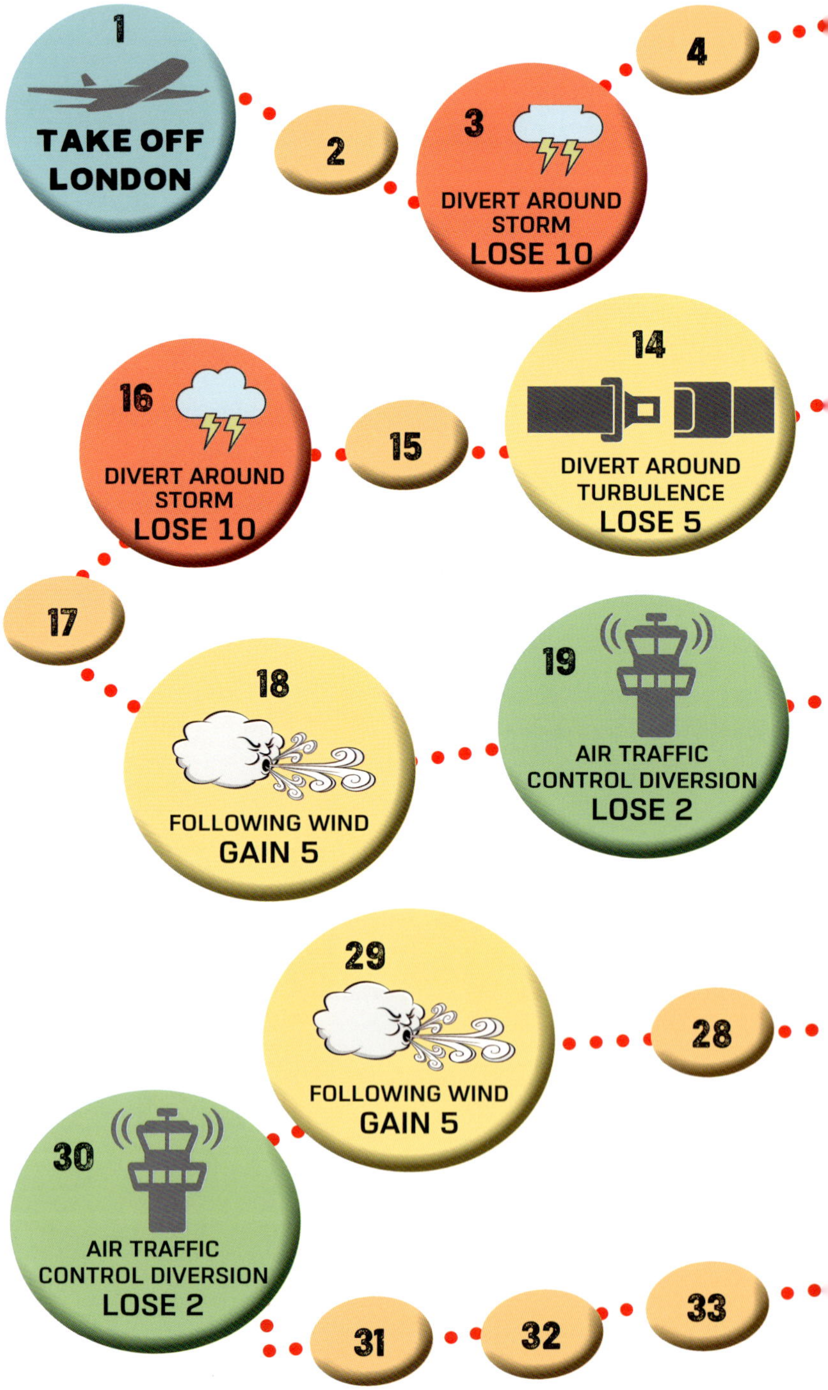

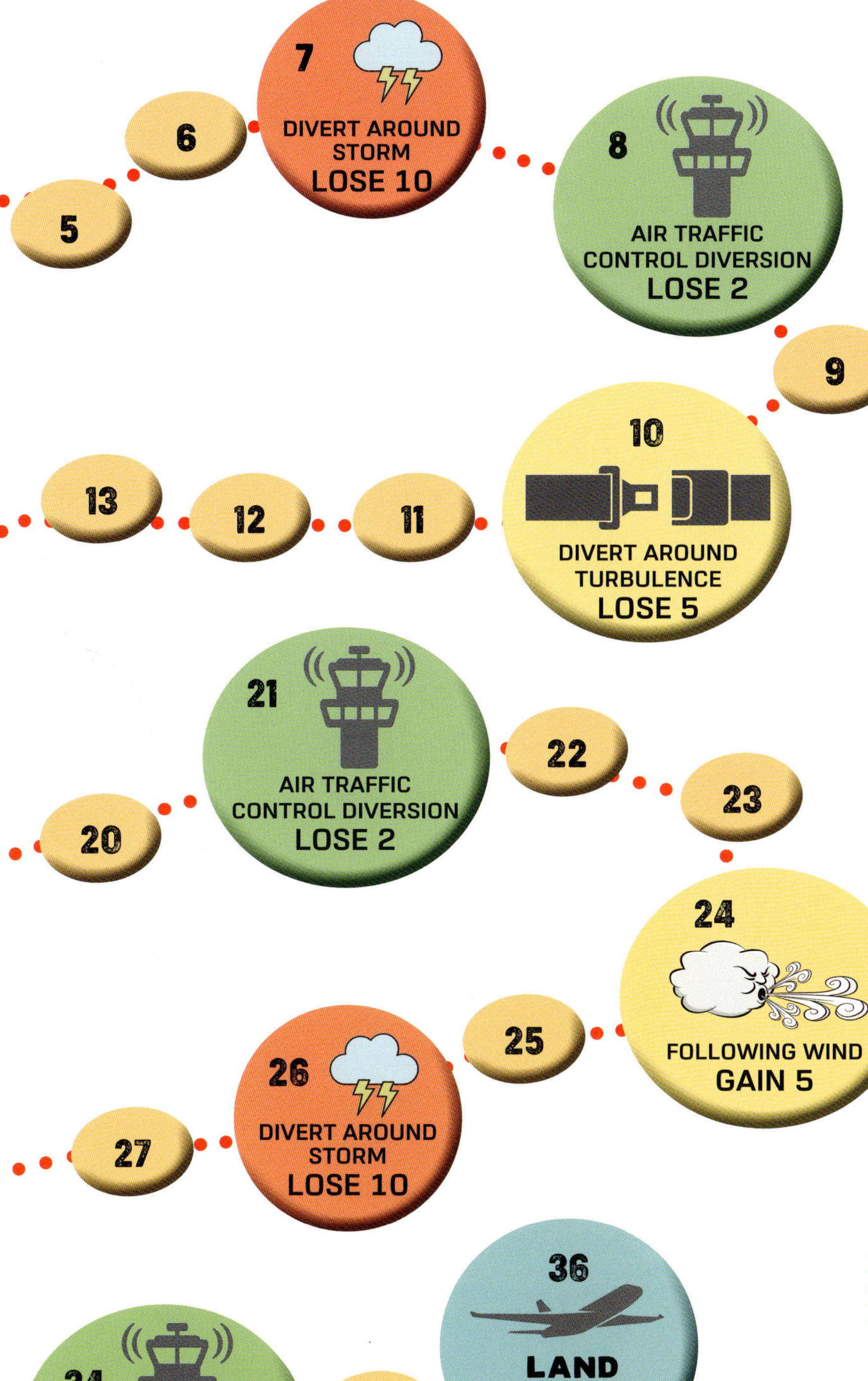

IN-FLIGHT CALCULATIONS

It is 10:30 pm and there are still 2,000 miles to fly to get to New York. The plane is travelling at 500 mph.

40 How much longer will the journey take?

41 What time will the plane land in New York?

The radar is showing a storm ahead. Flying around the storm, will add 250 miles to the journey.

42 How much longer will the flight take?

43 What time will the plane now land?

When you throw a dice you can't control what happens. This is a bit like bad weather— pilots have no control over the weather, but they have to be able to make calculations to deal with it.

A Change of Plan

Sometimes an aircraft cannot land at its planned destination. When this happens, the pilot has to make a quick decision about what to do. The time is 10:55 pm (22:55) and a plane is approaching JFK Aiport in New York. A terrible storm is in the area. JFK will be closed until 1:00 am (01:00). The pilot has to decide whether to circle (fly over) and wait for JFK to reopen or divert to a different airport.

45 **WHAT SHOULD THE PILOT DO?**

- **The aircraft uses 19,842 lb of fuel every hour.**
- **The in-flight computer shows 29,762 of fuel left.**
- **The clocks (below) show the current time.**

Which option should the pilot choose?

OPTION 1: Circle until JFK reopens at **1:00 am (01:00)** and land there.
OPTION 2: Fly to Boston Logan Airport which closes at **11:15 pm (23:15)**. It will take half an hour to fly to Boston.
OPTION 3: Fly to Washington Dulles Airport which closes at **11:45 pm (23:45)**. It will take **45 minutes** to fly to Washington Airport.

(You will find a TIP to help you with this activity on page 29 and information about 24 HOUR CLOCKS.)

Analogue clock

Digital clock

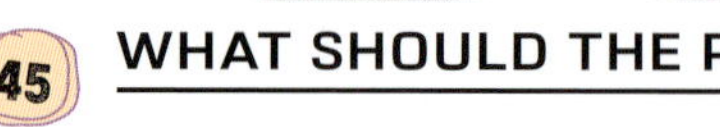

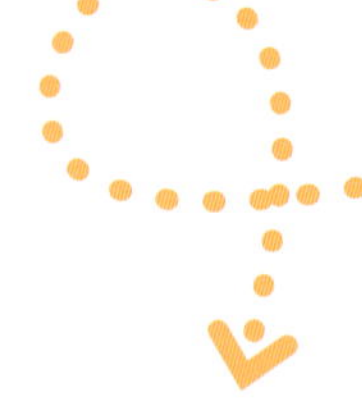

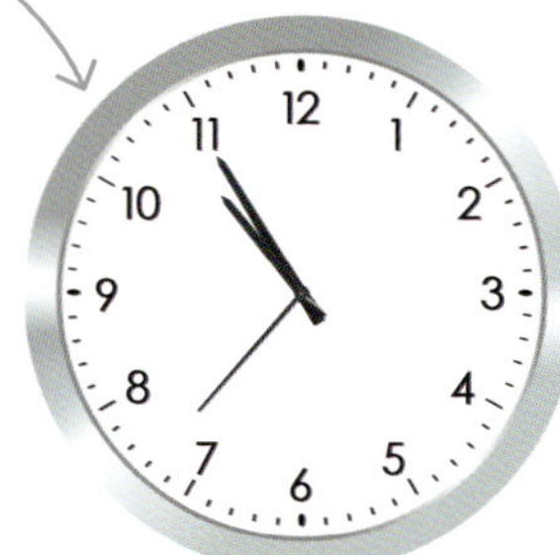

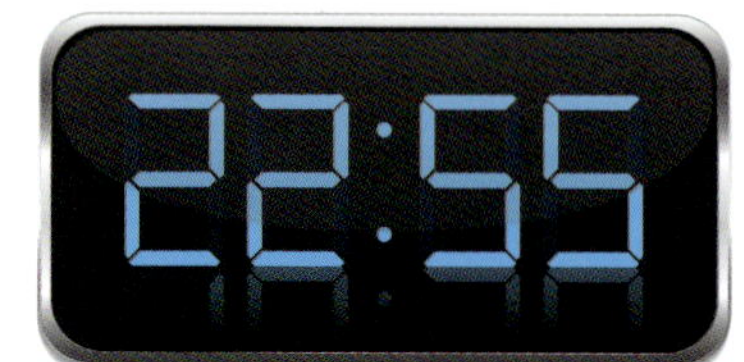

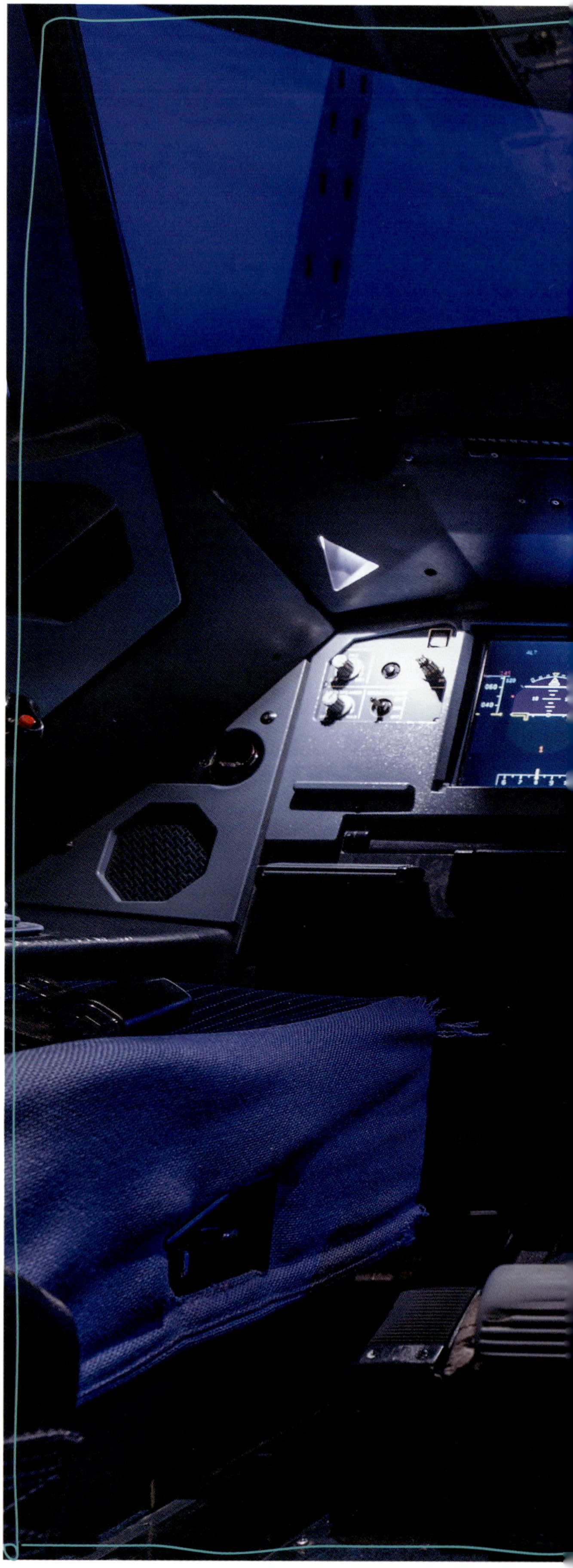

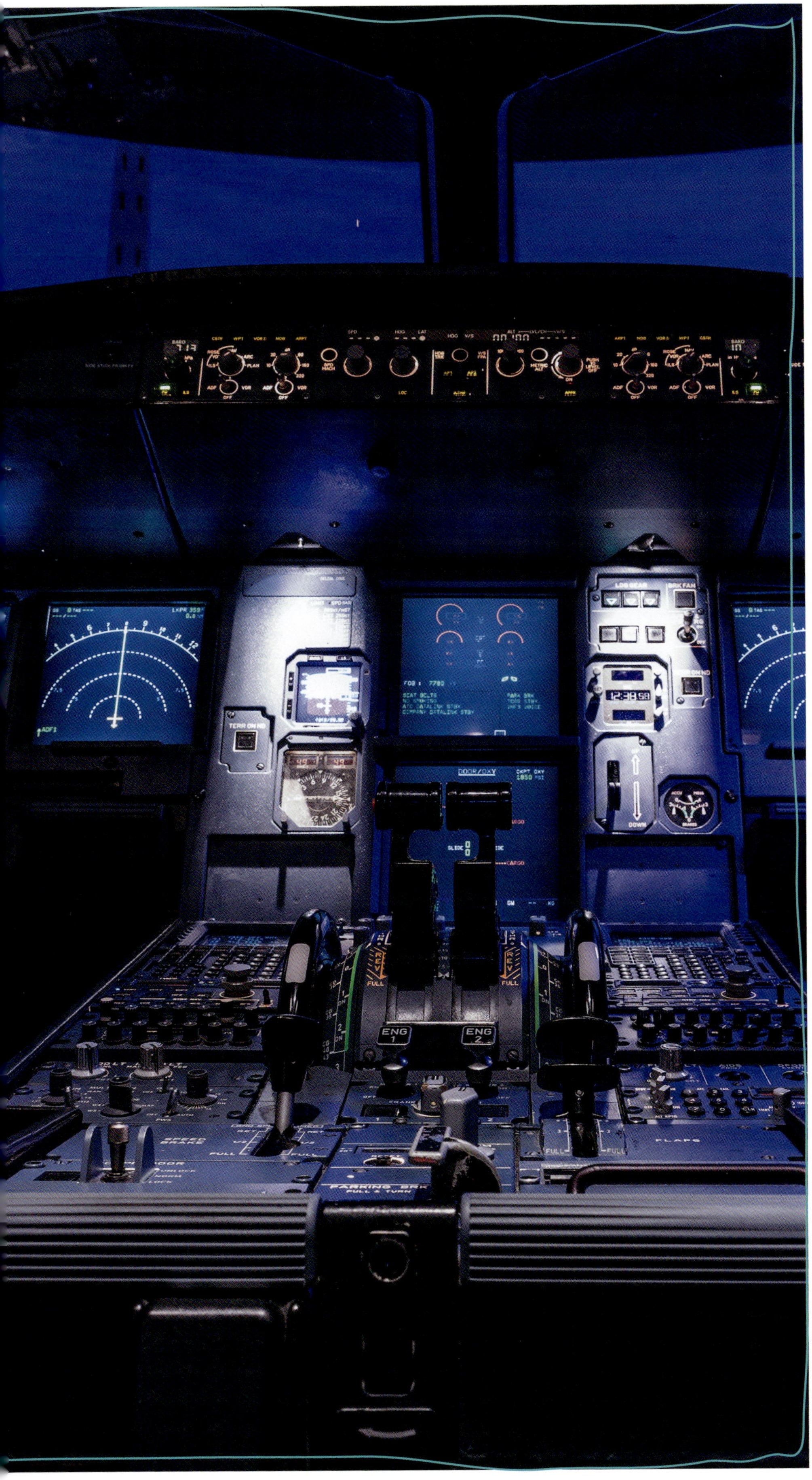

A380 FACTS

- An A380 airliner weighs the same as five blue whales.
- It can fly for 17 hours non-stop.
- An A380 can hold as many as 853 passengers—but most planes carry around 525 in three classes.
- Each plane has four engines, but the outer two engines on each wing can't go in reverse. They would kick up too much debris from the edge of the runways.

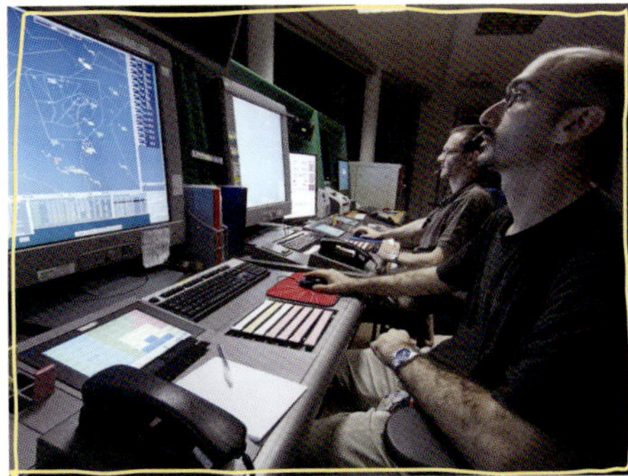

Air traffic controllers notify pilots of any weather problems at the airport

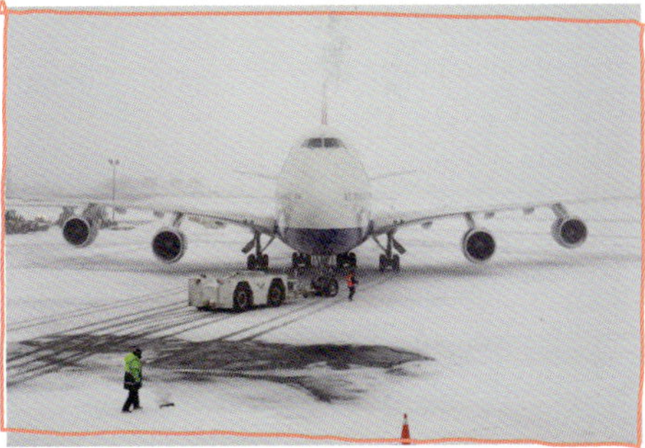

Ice and snow at JFK airport

46 HOW MUCH FUEL?

If the plane has to circle (fly over) New York for **two and a half hours,** how much fuel would be needed to do this?

Cleared to Land

The flight is nearly over. Storms, turbulence, and even an emergency diversion have been successfully negotiated. The captain has just told the crew to prepare for landing. The copilot has never landed at Washington Dulles Airport before, but the runway and the area around the airport is familar. This is because, in training, pilots practice landing at this and other airports in a flight simulator. The control tower has cleared the plane to land.

LANDING

The plane is cruising at an altitude (height) of 24,800 feet and is due to land in **seven minutes**. After one minute the plane has descended 4,800 feet and is at a lower altitude of 20,000 feet. The BAR LINE CHART shows the descent of the plane from this point. Use the chart to answer the questions below:

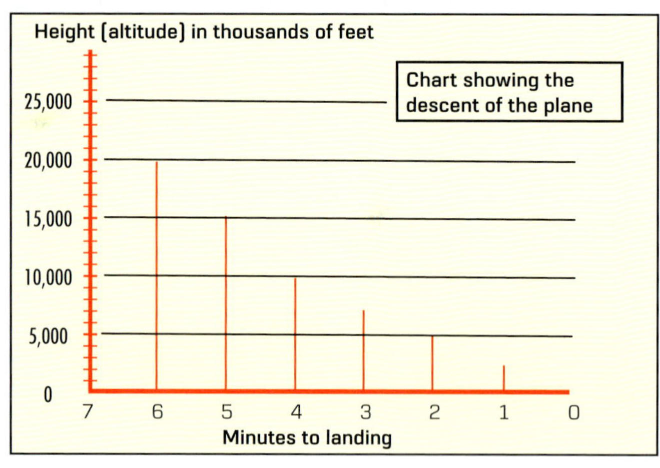

47 How high is the plane after descending for 2 minutes?

48 After how many minutes of descent has the plane reached 10,000 feet?

49 What is the height of the plane at 2 minutes before landing?

50 When the plane has reached 15,000 feet, how many minutes is it from landing?

51 What is the height of the plane at three minutes to landing?

(You will find a TIP to help you with these questions on page 29.)

PILOT FACT

Pilots are only allowed to fly for eight flying hours in a day, 100 flying hours in a month, and 1,000 flying hours in a year. Flights that are longer than eight hours are called long haul flights.

THE RUNWAY

The stopping distance for a plane on a dry runway is 2040 metres. On a wet runway it takes a plane an extra 304 metres to stop.

52 What is the wet runway stopping distance?

53 Now write your answer in millimetres.

(You will find information about UNITS OF MEASUREMENT on page 29.)

LANDING PROCEDURE

- The captain tells the crew to prepare for landing.
- The captain and copilot run through the landing briefing. This includes all the normal procedures and the actions to be taken if there is an emergency.
- The wing flaps and undercarriage (wheels) are lowered.
- The control tower at the airport clears the aircraft to land.
- Once the aircraft has passed over the start of the runway, the thrust levers are pulled back and the nose is lifted by pulling back on the controls. This makes sure that the plane lands on the stronger, main undercarriage.
- As an A380 touches down, it is travelling at 160 mph.

On the Ground

The plane has landed at Washington Dulles International Airport. It has flown a total of 3,672 miles and the aircraft has burnt the equivelant of 17,153 gallons of fuel. In an average family car this would be enough fuel to drive from the Earth to the Moon, back to the Earth and then back to the Moon again! Pilots must be able to read maps and charts. Using the grid map below, see what you can find at the airport.

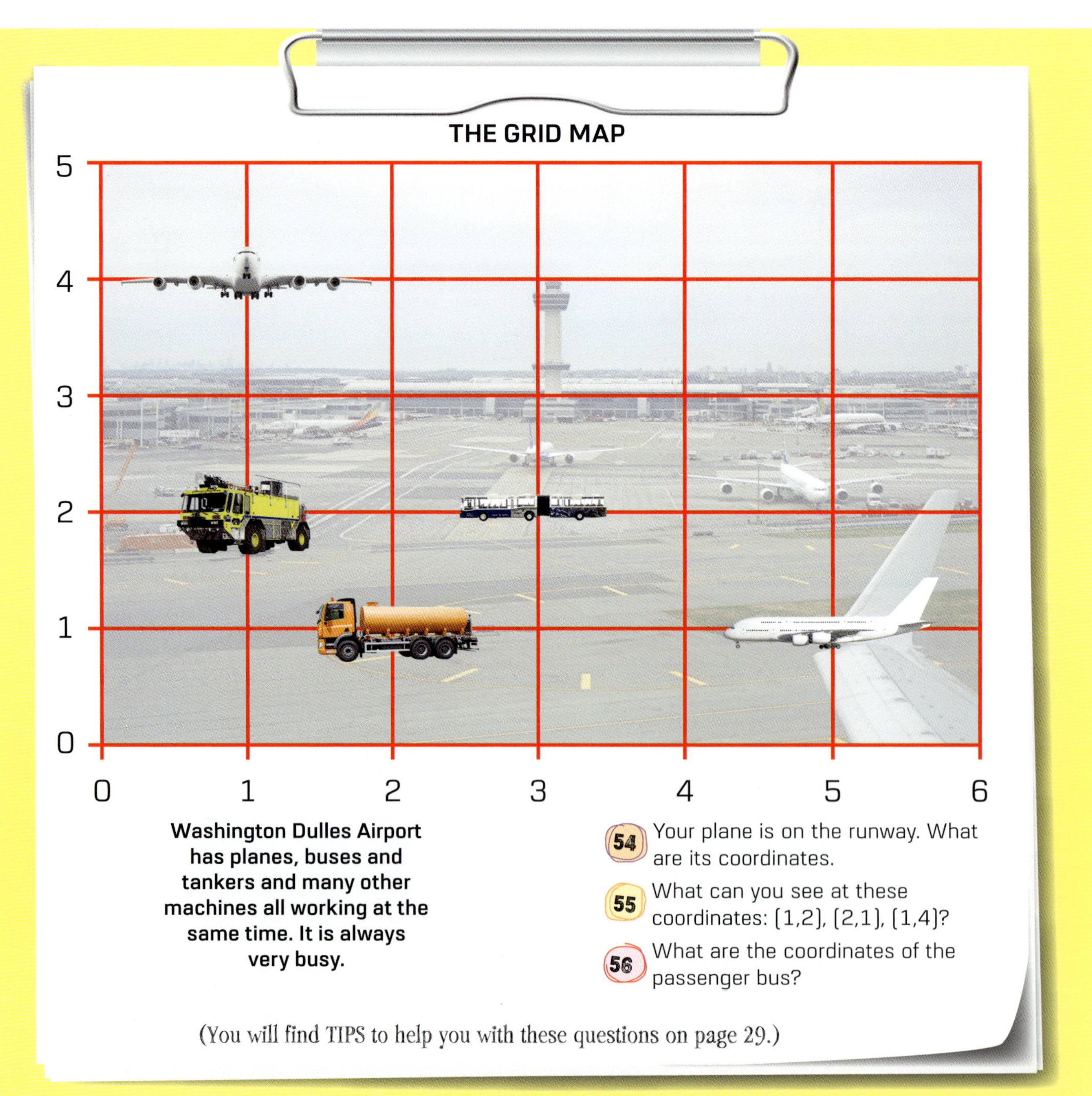

Washington Dulles Airport has planes, buses and tankers and many other machines all working at the same time. It is always very busy.

54 Your plane is on the runway. What are its coordinates.

55 What can you see at these coordinates: (1,2), (2,1), (1,4)?

56 What are the coordinates of the passenger bus?

(You will find TIPS to help you with these questions on page 29.)

BAGGAGE

The baggage handlers have a number of parcels to unload and they all have different shapes.

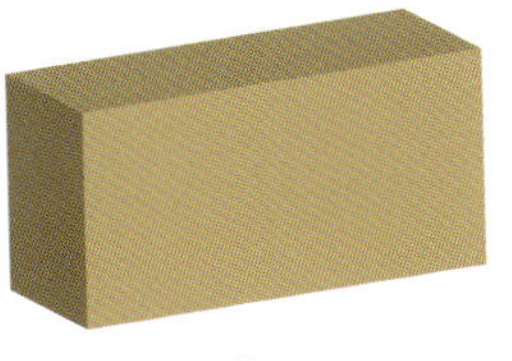

A

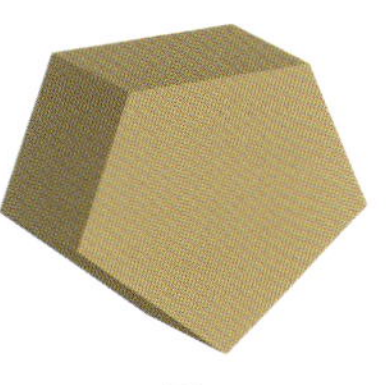

B

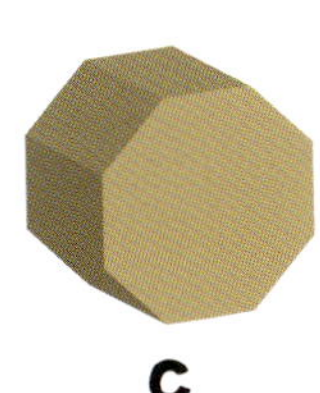

C

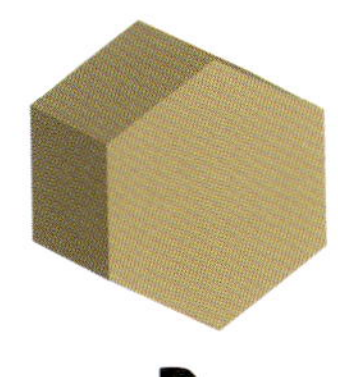

D

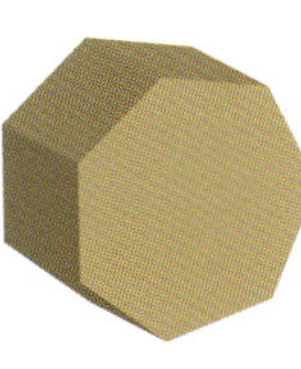

E

57 Name the shape which has four RIGHT ANGLES?

58 Name the shape which has two pairs of sides of equal length?

59 Which REGULAR shape can be made from six identical EQUILATERAL TRIANGLES?

60 Find the shapes with seven and eight sides. What are they called?

61 In which shape can you join all the corners to make a star with a PENTAGON in its centre?

CARGO FACT

The NOTAC (Notification to Captain) is a document that tells the captain about any special or dangerous cargo that may be on board.

AT THE AIRPORT

An A380 has two decks for passengers and a third for baggage and cargo. The baggage is loaded into small containers and placed in the aircraft. In the image above, baggage and catering are being loaded on to the three decks at the same time.

Tips for Math Success

FUEL CAPACITY

Reading and writing large numbers

TIP: When reading or listening to the names of large numbers, such as "fifteen thousand, eight hundred and six", it helps to write the number down using digits like this: "15,806."

AIRPORT FACTS

Interpreting a bar chart
A bar chart (also called a bar graph) shows quantities and the size of things.

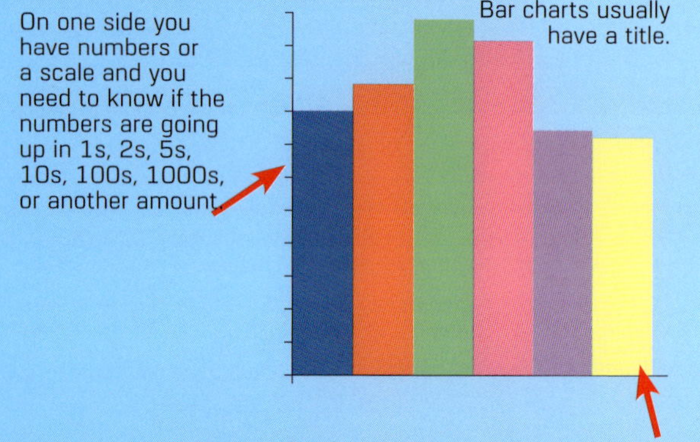

The heights of the bars on the bar chart on page 8 show numbers of passengers passing through airports every year. If the red bar is Los Angeles International Airport, then you know that this bar shows 56,000,000 passengers. Look at the heights of the other bars in turn and match them to the numbers of passengers in the DATA BOX.

NUMBER OF PASSENGERS

TIP: There are 52 weeks in a year.

PREFLIGHT TASKS

Understanding division
Fractions and division are related. For example, finding a half of a thing or a number, is the same as dividing it by two.
If you know a multiplication then you also know some other related facts. For example: **15 x 4 = 60** and from this we know that **60 ÷ 15 = 4**

THE FLIGHT PLAN

TIP: There are 60 minutes in one hour.

THE CARGO HOLD

Imagining 3-D shapes
TIP: If you find it difficult to imagine the shapes made by the stacks of cube-shaped boxes, get some small blocks and try making the shapes.

HOW FAR?

Calculations
TIP: Before doing any calculation decide what sort of calculation it is: addition, subtraction, division, or multiplication?
For example, if a plane travels 300 miles in one hour, and you need to find out how far it travels in one minute, you need to divide 300 by 60 (minutes).

FOOD AND DRINK

Comparing numbers
Here are the meanings for the symbols:
> means greater than < means less than

For example: 16 – 3 > 99 – 95
$\frac{1}{4}$ < 0.5

WHAT SHOULD THE PILOT DO

TIP: If you are going to circle New York you need enough fuel for 2 hours 5 minutes of flight.

Using a 24 hour clock

You will notice that the times in brackets have been given using a 24 hour clock. Look at the analogue clocks. In 24 hours (a day and a night), the hour hand travels twice around the clock face.

ANALOGUE CLOCKS	DIGITAL CLOCKS

06:00

6:00 am

18:00

6:00 pm

• 6 o'clock

03:30

3:30 am

15:30

3:30 pm

• Half past three
• Three thirty

TIP: 'am' means before noon (in the morning) and 'pm' means after noon.

LANDING

A bar line chart has lines rather than bars. To read a bar line chart you need to look at the tops of the lines and the scale at the side to interpret where the lines reach.

THE GRID MAP

Using coordinates:

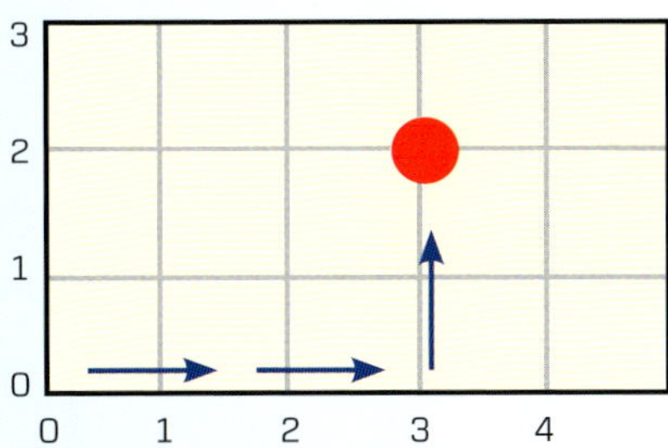

To find the coordinates of a point on a grid, you read along the bottom of the grid first, then up the side of the grid.

For example, a grid reference of **(3,2)** means **3 steps** along the bottom then **2 steps** up to find the exact point.

UNITS OF MEASUREMENT

There are two main systems of measurement across the world: metric (such as centimetres, metres, kilometres, grams, kilograms) and imperial (such as inches, feet, miles, ounces, pounds).

METRIC		IMPERIAL	
Length		**Length**	
1 millimetre (mm)		1 inch (in)	
1 centimetre (cm)	= 10 mm	1 foot (ft)	= 12 in
1 metre (m)	= 100 cm	1 yard (yd)	= 3 ft
1 kilometre (km)	= 1000 m	1 mile	= 1760 yd
Weight		**Weight**	
1 gram (g)		1 ounce (oz)	
1 kilogram (kg)	= 1000 g	1 pound (lb)	= 16 oz
Capacity		**Capacity**	
1 millilitre (ml)		1 fluid ounce (fl oz)	
1 centilitre (cl)	= 10 ml	1 US pint (pt)	= 16 fl oz
1 litre (l)	= 1000 ml	1 US gallon (gal)	= 8 US pt

Comparing metric and imperial measurements

1 kilometre = 0.62 of a mile

1 kilogram = 2.20 pounds

0.47 litre = 1 US pint

Answers

PAGES 6–7

ASSESSING THE PILOT CADET

1) The aircraft programmed into the flight simulator is the Boeing 737.

FUEL CAPACITY

2) The maximum fuel capacity of the Airbus A320 is b) Five thousand, two hundred and forty eight gallons.

PAGES 8–9

AIRPORT FACTS

3) The **bar chart** shows the following numbers of passengers:
- Blue bar: 80,000,000 London Heathrow UK
- Red bar: 88,000,000 Los Angeles International
- Green bar: 107,000,000 Hartsfield International Atlanta USA
- Pink bar: 101,000,000 Beijing Shunyi China
- Purple and yellow bars: 74,000,000 Shanghai China and 72,000,000 Paris Charles De Gaulle

NUMBER OF PASSENGERS

4) You need to divide the passenger numbers by 52 to find out how many passengers go through each airport in a week.

PAGES 10–11

PREFLIGHT TASKS

5) 11 tyres need replacing.
6) 10 ladders.
7) Each cleaner cleans 55 windows.
8) 34,675 gallons.
9) 628 in-flight magazines are needed.

THE WALK-AROUND

10) 762 feet has been walked.

The length of the plane	240 ft
Twice the **wingspan** (2 x 261 ft)	+ 522 ft
	762 ft

PAGES 12–13

THE FLIGHT PLAN

11) 470 miles further.
12) 50 minutes difference.
13) You will travel 2,579 miles.
14) You will travel 7,859 miles.
15) The total journey time is 14 hours and 10 minutes.

WHICH CITY

16) Atlanta and Los Angeles
17) Moscow.
18) Rome and Cairo.

PAGES 14–15

CHECKING THE FUEL

19) 158,640 lbs of fuel
20) 13,220 lbs of fuel
21) 19,830 lbs of fuel

CARGO HOLD

22)

23)

HOW HEAVY?

24] The weight of the plane and its fuel is 1,157,420 lb.
25] The maximum that the cargo, passengers, and crew can weigh is 77,168 lbs.
26] After 5 minutes, you will be 15,000 ft high.
27] After 10 minutes, you will be 30,000 ft high.
28] After 12 minutes, the plane's altitude is 36,000 ft.

HOW FAR?

29] 7 miles in one minute.
30] 84 miles in 12 minutes.

IN-FLIGHT SERVICE

31] 242 bottles	32] 3000 ml (3 litres)
33] 200 cartons	34] 13,500 ml (13.5 litres)
35] 114 bottles	36] True
37] True	38] False

A CUP OF COFFEE

39] 10 pots of coffee.
40] 10 litres.

IN-FLIGHT CALCULATIONS

41] 4 hours
42] 2:30 am
43] Half an hour (30 minutes) longer
44] 3:00 am

WHAT SHOULD THE PILOT DO?

45] The correct choice is option 3: Fly to Washington Dulles Airport.

(Option 1 is wrong because you would need just over 39,683 lb of fuel to circle for 2 hours and 5 minutes. Option 2 is wrong because Boston Logan Airport closes in 20 minutes and it will take you 30 minutes to fly there.)

HOW MUCH FUEL?

46] You would need 49,605 lb of fuel to fly (circle) for two and a half hours.

LANDING

47] 15,000 feet	48] 3 minutes
49] 5,000 feet	50] 5 minutes
51] 7,500 feet (approximately)	

THE RUNWAY

52] The wet runway stopping distance is 2,344 metres.
53] 2,344,000 millilitres

THE GRID MAP

54] (5,1)

55] (1,2) Fire engine
(2,1) Fuel tanker
(1,4) Plane taking off

56] (3,2)

57] The rectangle (A) has four right angles.

58] The rectangle (A) has two pairs of sides of equal length.

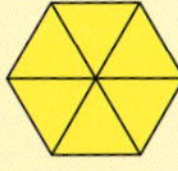

59] The regular hexagon (D) can be made from six identical equilateral triangles.

BAGGAGE

60] (E) the heptagon has seven sides.
(C) the octagon has eight sides.

61] You can join all the corners of a pentagon (shape B) to make a star with a pentagon in its center.

Glossary

AERODYNAMICS The study of how solid things move through the air.

AIR TRAFFIC CONTROLLERS People who work in air traffic control. ATCs make sure that planes stay a safe distance apart in the sky. They inform pilots about the weather and other problems, and they organise the flow of planes in and out of airports.

CABIN Where the passengers sit in an aircraft.

COCKPIT The area at the front of the plane where the pilots sit.

COMMERCIAL AIRLINERS Planes that carry people or cargo for money.

CONTROL TOWER The airport building where the air traffic controllers work.

CRUISING SPEED A steady, constant speed that a plane flies at when it has reached its flying level.

FLIGHT INSTRUMENTS The mechanical and electrical devices used for flying the plane.

FLIGHT PLAN A detailed plan of a plane's journey, showing where the plane will fly, the length of the flight, how much fuel will be used, the plane's speed, and the expected weather conditions.

FLIGHT SIMULATORS Machines that use computer programs to create real-life flying conditions. Pilots train and practice in flight simulators.

FUEL CAPACITY The amount of fuel a plane can carry.

FUSELAGE The central body section of a plane.

METEOROLOGY Studying weather.

NAVIGATION Working out the best route for an aircraft to take.

RADAR A method of detecting distant objects or weather using radio waves.

RANGE The distance a plane can fly without refuelling.

STATUTE MILES The official way of saying "miles." Pilots use this term.

THRUST A pushing force created in a jet engine, giving the plane enough speed to take off.

TURBULENCE Strong currents of rising and falling air. Turbulence can make a flight bumpy.

WINGSPAN The distance between the tips of the wings of an aircraft.

MATHS GLOSSARY

BAR CHART A chart or graph with bars of the same width that can be used to compare numbers or size of things against a scale.

BAR LINE CHART This chart shows information in lines. The height of the line can be read against the scale on the chart.

CUBE A regular 3-D shape with six square faces.

EQUILATERAL TRIANGLES Triangles with all three sides equal in length.

FRACTIONS These are made when shapes or numbers are cut into equal parts. For example, if a shape is cut into four equal parts, each part is one whole divided by four, or a quarter [¼].

HEPTAGON A 2-D shape with seven sides.

HEXAGON A 2-D shape with six sides.

MASS in everyday life, mass is often called weight.

PENTAGON A 2-D shape with five sides.

REGULAR Used to describe 2-D shapes which have sides that are equal in length and 3-D shapes with faces all the same in shape and size.

RIGHT ANGLE A quarter of a whole turn or revolution, measured in degrees. A right angle is 90 degrees [90°].

VOLUME The amount of space something takes up or how much it holds, for example, the amount of liquid a bottle holds.

Picture Credits.

extNewMedia, Robert Sarosiek, Steve Mann, travellight, Nadezda Murmakova. 8-9: Thomas Barrat, Katherine Welles. 10-1: Skycolors, Agent Wolf. 12-13: Eugenius777, dikobraziy, logoboom, Chaay_Tee, Dmitry Naumov, Catarina Belova, TTstudio, rayints, Fourleaflover. 14-15: Sorbis, Belish. 16-17: tostphoto, Sarunyu L, Ryan Fletcher. 18-19: Cromo Digital, Dmitry Birin, Agent Wolf, Sorbis. 20-21: Mark1987, Demja, 13ree.design, John T Takai, vladwel. 22-23: Nadezda Murmakova, firstpentuer_3.30o,Clock, firstpentuer, PixMarket, Angelo Giampiccolo. 24-25: Skycolors, Petr Akulin. 26-27: ymgerman, SVStudio, Dobresum, urbanbuzz, Ioan Panaite, EQRoy.

Every effort has been made to trace the copyright holders, and we apologize in advance for any unintentional omissions. We would be pleased to insert the appropriate acknowledgements in any subsequent edition of this publication.